Can You Hear Me Now?
Does God Still Speak?

By Billie Gorham

"I spoke to you, rising up early and speaking,
but you didn't hear me; I called you, but you didn't answer."
Jeremiah 7:13

Twenty-Four Lessons Learned by Listening

Print ISBN: 978-1-54395-013-7

eBook ISBN: 978-1-54395-014-4

INTRODUCTION

Have you ever wondered where God is sometimes? Does it seem as if your prayers are not getting past the ceiling? Do you think to yourself, "I am not sure that God hears me and I am definitely not thinking that I can hear Him, if He does still speak. It feels like one of those advertisements that we had on TV when cell phones first came out, "Can you hear me now? Can you hear me now?"

When He first started talking to me, I would often think it was my imagination. But when strange words popped into my head, words I sometimes had to look up in the dictionary,0 I began to figure out that Someone was trying to tell me something. His Words in the Bible had always spoken to me and I would often ask Him to verify what I was hearing by showing it to me in His Word. I didn't want to start a new religion or believe that I was a fanatical neurotic.

I write this book with a little trepidation. I don't want anyone to think I see myself as super- spiritual and I would rather no one consider me completely crazy. My family and friends who already know I am weird might be too easily convinced. One of my friends gave me a calendar that pretty well sums me up: "Pretending to be a normal person day after day is exhausting." I am just a person who can testify, without concern for what anyone else thinks, that God still speaks.

God speaks in the sun, the universe, and the beauty of creation. If we stop and look, we know that God is and we are astonished at His handiwork.

Does He speak audibly? I think so. I yearn to hear His voice audibly, as Moses, Isaiah, Elijah, and other prophets did. But I have had Him speak, often, to my spirit and He has done things in my life that I could have never dreamed up.

That is why I have written this little book. It is a book about learning to listen so that you can hear God when He speaks. I am still working at it.

Psalm 66: 18,19. "If I regard iniquity in my heart, the Lord will not hear me; But verily God hath heard me; he hath attended to the voice of my prayer."

TABLE OF CONTENTS

RECOGNIZE HIS PRESENCE!

One of the most impressive individuals in the Bible to me is Enoch, the father of Methuselah, because he and God enjoyed their walks together so much that one day God just took him home with Him. I love to feel the presence of God's Holy Spirit surround me and I can't wait to walk with Jesus right up to the throne of God. But, if you want to recognize His presence here on earth, you will need to take some time to wait, worship and walk with Him.

"I'll Never Walk Alone"

My father considered himself an entrepreneur. Looking back, I think he was a gambler who was always looking for a way to get rich. He was also my hero. I cannot tell you why. Perhaps when I was small, he gave me the attention that he would have given to a boy but with two more babies following quickly, he had no time to give me much favoritism. He was a salesman, with an out-going personality who always made me laugh.

Even after he came back from the navy, tall and handsome in his sailor outfit, he was never home for one reason or another and, when he was home, he and Mother argued all the time. I remember many times when my two sisters and I cried outside their bedroom door, pleading with them to stop yelling at each other.

When he left us, Mother had to find a way to make a living so she got a job as a telephone operator. When she saw a chance to get farther away, she transferred to a little town in North Texas. Alone, she took us on a bus, away from family and friends, without a car, a home, or money. It was many years before I realized how very brave she was.

I was the typical rebellious child. I just knew it was my Mom's fault that I had to leave my friends, our home, our family and I even blamed her for Daddy leaving us. I think it would have been worse had it not been for the fact that we found a church where we went every time the doors opened. Mother made sure of that, even when she was working crazy hours at the telephone company.

Often she had to work nights and she took us with her. She would clear off the desks and the chairs and let us sleep there. I had the longest desk since I was a tall ten-year-old and I still remember how hard that desk was.

We never went hungry and we always knew she would take care of us, no matter what. But we wouldn't always have what we wanted and we never got by with anything. She believed in discipline, she demanded obedience and she always expected us to do our best.

Five years later, when she remarried, I really rebelled. Her new husband brought in a son who was my age, thirteen, and a daughter, who was my sister's age, twelve, into a two-bedroom, one-bath house. They enclosed the porch for his son but it still meant that four girls would have to share one bedroom. It was wall to wall beds. I was okay with the daughter but I wasn't crazy about a boy being in the house. I also hated the idea of sharing our mother with her new husband.

To be alone, I got into the habit of walking the oil fields behind our house. Even at night, when I could see only by the moonlight, I could walk almost to the Red River, which divides Texas and Oklahoma. That was when I first felt Jesus walking with me. I did most of the talking, probably complaining. But He was there, listening. No matter how late the hour or how dark the night, I never was afraid. He was there. God was walking with me.

A few years later, on the day I married, I tried to sing a solo. I say tried because, although I had sung in the choir for years, I couldn't sing well and since it was my wedding day, I was extremely nervous. After much hesitation and some help from the choir director, I finally, to the relief of the church members, finished the song. That day I had chosen to sing "I'll walk with God from this day on," because (one,) I have always been overly dramatic, and (two,) I recognized how important my time walking through the oil fields had been. I vowed, for the rest of my life, to continue to walk with God.

Psalm 23:4 "Even though I walk through the darkest valley, I will fear no evil, for you are with me."

TEST THE WORD!

The Bible says that wives should submit to their husbands, (Eph. 5:22.) I have not always liked that verse and often I demanded my own way. But, if you want to be sure that you are hearing from God, you have to follow His rule book.

"College Crazy"

My husband was twenty-one and I was seventeen on the day we married. Madly in love, I never thought that I would want to do anything but just bask in his presence all day, every day. (It is amazing how fast you tire of basking.)

But truthfully, I had been busy enough finishing high school, working at the local telephone company, and having four children. (Three of them were in diapers at the same time and those were before disposable diapers.) The youngest was about a month old when I got the wild-hair notion that I wanted to go to college.

"College!" my husband shouted, "With four babies, you do not have time for college and we certainly do not have the money!"

After a bit of hostile discussion, he ended the subject with, "If you had wanted to go to college, you should have married one of those lawyers on the other side of town!"

Not knowing why I felt such a compulsion to go to college and realizing that he was right about not having the time or money, I went back to the kitchen. Knowing the Bible says, "Knock and the door will be opened to you," I said to God, "Lord, I think that door just got slammed shut, so, if you want me to go, you will have to open it again. If you want me to get a college degree, let Weldon decide that it is a good idea." Then I dropped it.

A few days later, Weldon said, "I've been thinking about you going to college. I've decided that it might be a good idea. We can't afford enough insurance to protect you and the kids if something happened to me, so with a degree, you could get a good job if it was ever necessary."

Most of the time I went from eight in the morning until nine at night, two days a week, working in fifteen hours each semester. I studied from ten at night, (after Weldon and the kids went to bed,) until two or three in the morning. Four and a half years and another baby later, I graduated from college. It had been long days, short nights and many rough times, but I know the Lord opened the door to college and He was the One who carried me through it.

Psalm 37:5 "Commit your way to the Lord; trust also in him and he will do this."

MAKE THE TIME!

Jesus was surrounded and hounded by people all day, every day and it was very difficult for him to get alone to pray. So He went out and spent all night talking to His Father, restoring His strength and power. Power comes with prayer.

"Are You Running With Me, Jesus?"

It was hard to find time for much prayer and Bible study when I had five children, a husband, parents, in-laws, out-laws, various relatives, a job, and college, so I was always running out the door asking, "Lord Jesus, will you run with me because as you can see, I am pretty busy? I want to be with you. I want to have fellowship with you, but there never seems to be any time. I am so sorry, again!"

It isn't that I didn't stay on my knees, I did,----- looking for shoes, (I needed 12 per day,) and I was always praying, "Lord, you know I need that shoe."

He always showed me where they were. That might have seemed small to other people, but believe me, it was a big thing to me.

One day, after I had found the twelfth shoe by praying, "Lord, please help me find that shoe so we can all get to school halfway on time," and then herding everyone to the car, I was again asking, "Lord Jesus, please, will you run with me today?"

I heard a gentle voice in my spirit say, "Yes, I am with you always, and, yes, when you are running, I run with you and I hear you. But, if you really want to hear me, you need to slow down and take time to sit at my feet and spend some time listening."

That got my attention! So, very sporadically, I started taking time to just sit, wait and listen. To be honest, an awful lot of those conversations happened in the bathroom. (It was the only place with a lock on the door.)

The hardest thing in the world is to wait. Since the advent of the microwave anything that takes longer than two minutes is not worth it. We are impatient people. We want instant gratification. We cannot wait for our mail to go across the country in two days because we have instant email. If anything sent to me takes longer than a minute to download, I say, "Forget it." We don't have time to call, we can text.

So many times we are like foolish children who say, "I'd rather do it myself" and then we run to him because we have messed up so badly. Like the time that I thought it would be so nice for my family to renovate a bathroom for a handicapped friend. I didn't ask God, I just plunged right in, removed the tub, re-arranged the commode and re-placed the linoleum with ceramic tile. Only afterward did I hear the health care providers say that it would have been easier for her if I had done it differently. In the middle of it all, I could only say, "I'm sorry, Lord. Would you please help me never to do this again without asking you how?"

Remembering what Jesus said that morning when He spoke was pretty easy because it caught me by surprise. But the waiting was not easy, so I started writing down my prayers, my thoughts, His answers and His words. It was one of the most encouraging things I have ever done. I have boxes full of notebooks that tell about all of the answered prayers and my conversations with God. It is awesome to look back and see how faithful God has been, how many prayers He has answered.

I remember one easily. A friend of mine had become very ill with pancreatitis. My journal shows that many times the Holy Spirit would tell me specifically how to pray for her. One morning, He said to pray for her head to be healed. I thought that was strange because it had nothing to do with pancreatitis, but I prayed. Later, when I contacted a member of the family, I was told that my friend had fallen that morning and hit her head and they were afraid that she had a concussion. Thankfully, the x-rays showed no damage. Oh, to always hear that clearly!

Isa. 49:23 "They shall not be ashamed that wait for me."

IT IS WORTH WAITING

It is strange to me that so many churches skip the parts of Acts that talk about being filled with the Holy Spirit. That is what changed those disciples from a bunch of wimps to people willing to die for their faith. The disciples had been fearfully waiting and the Holy Spirit blew in and transformed them. I want to be that changed, that different. But, it has to do with waiting.

"The Filling Station"

I was asking the Lord how I could become more Spirit-filled because it seemed like nothing spiritual was happening in my life, in my family, in my church. I had been a born-again Christian since I was a child but as I grew older, I hungered for His presence, His power. I knew I had the Holy Spirit in me but I had read of a baptism by the Holy Spirit with evidence of speaking in tongues, just like in Acts, and I wanted it.

Ephesians 5:18 "And be not drunk with wine, wherein is excess; but be filled with the Spirit."

The summer that I was studying for an Administrator's Certificate, I spent two weeks on the seventh floor of a university dormitory by myself. Everyone else was on the first two floors. I had not planned that and it was scary but I was determined to search for the presence of God. I read about the Holy Spirit and prayed, able to sleep only with the help of Bible tapes.

In the middle of the two weeks, I came home and went to a Pentecostal church, seeking the baptism. A woman stood and spoke in tongues. Another woman interpreted and what she said described me and what I was going through at that time. Afterward I went to the front, someone prayed over me, and nothing happened.

Two weeks later, when I was driving down the road, suddenly words came out of my mouth that sounded like nothing I had ever heard. I wondered, "Could that be the baptism …?" Not sure of what was happening, I spoke more and more unintelligible words.

It just made me hungrier, so I asked, "Lord Jesus, how do I get more of your Spirit."

He told me, "It is easy. See that filling station." I was passing Alexander's Station at the time. He said, "When you pull in there, you expect to get filled up. But if you pull right back out, you will not get enough gas to go very far.

If you pull into my "Filling Station" and if you will stay awhile, I will fill up your tank with the Holy Spirit. "The longer you stay and wait, the more I will fill you."

The analogy seemed to go further in my thoughts. "I will also clean your windows by washing you with the Word so that you can see more clearly. I will clean your whole vehicle of its insults and hurts and I will vacuum out the trash that is inside that has been there so long that you do not even realize it's there."

"If you take time, I will make sure that you stay at a correct temperature, instead of going hot and cold. I will also check your tires and make sure that they are aired up so that your ride will be smoother no matter what road you are traveling."

"If you come in early in the day, you will not have to worry about running out of gas and your day will definitely go better. Even if a problem comes up, I will be on call and will be happy to come and fix it. You can depend on 24-hour service, always with a smile."

"They that wait upon the Lord shall renew their strength, they shall mount up with wings as eagles, they shall run and not be weary, they shall walk and not faint." Isa. 40:31

His Filling Station is the best place in the world. It is my "Hiding Place."

Although I cannot sing or play an instrument, Jesus gave me this song, words and music. I did not realize it at the time but it is based on Psalms 32:7, "You are my hiding place; you will preserve me from trouble; you will surround me with songs of deliverance."

THE HIDING PLACE

There is a hiding place, a quiet holy place,
Where no one comes to me, except my Lord.
He is my Hiding Place, a refuge from the storm,
I trust in Him, the Spirit and the Word.
No matter where I've been, how deep in sin I'm in,
His love will draw me with a silken cord,
To find the hiding place, where no one sees my face,
Except the precious Savior, Christ the Lord.

How could He die for me, alone, upon the tree,
To give us vict'try, all the human race?
It was tremendous love, flowing from heav'n above,
And it is found in this, the hiding place.
If you want peace within, a joy that's never been,
A love that draws you with a silken cord,
Then find the hiding place, where no one sees your face,
Except the precious Savior, Christ the Lord.

The Lord said to me one day when I was complaining about never having enough time, "Billie, when my word says, 'I can do all things through Christ who strengthens me,' I did not mean that you had to try to do ALL things."

DO IT NOW!

God told Ananias to go find a man called Saul of Tarsus. Now, Ananias knew Saul's reputation and wasn't too excited about going to someone who had persecuted the saints all over Israel. God sent him anyway because he had a plan for Saul. Saul, the persecutor would soon become Paul, the preacher, because Ananias heard and obeyed.

"Flowers for a Lady"

One morning I was at the grocery store buying the weeks' worth of groceries, which I knew, with my bunch, would not last two days, and I was passing an area which was filled with potted mums. Suddenly I was impressed to buy a pot of mums and take it to an older woman who had been our neighbor when we lived in town. I thought, "Okay, Lord, as soon as I finish buying groceries."

He said, "Do it now."

I said, "Okay," left my cart in the middle of the aisle, picked up a pot of beautiful mums, paid for them and drove to Mrs. Johnson's house

Now, this lady was a saint of the church, a teacher of the Bible and a very intelligent, wise woman. She had lost her husband and was living with her granddaughter's family but she still had her confidence and joy.

I knocked on the door. No one came to answer it, so I thought, "I guess I heard you wrong, Lord." Turning to leave, I walked by the front window and heard someone crying. Backing up, I knocked and opened the door a little and called, "Mrs. Johnson, it's Billie. May I come in?" Still, all I could hear was crying.

Walking into the living room, I saw poor little Mrs. Johnson, sitting in a chair, sobbing so hard she was shaking.

I asked, "What in the world has happened? Why are you so upset?"

She looked surprised to see me. Then she started trying to tell me, between sobs, "I am going to Hell."

"Oh, Mrs. Johnson," I replied, "if you are going to Hell, the rest of us have no chance."

"No, I committed the unpardonable sin and I cannot go to Heaven."

"What do you mean?"

"When the children came in from their church and were telling me about the things that happened there, I made fun of them. I realize now that I was ridiculing the Holy Spirit and that is the unpardonable sin, so I cannot go to Heaven."

I knew the verse that she was talking about. Jesus said in Matthew 12:32, "And whosoever speaks a word against the Son of man, it shall be forgiven him: but whosoever speaks against the Holy Ghost, it shall not be forgiven him, neither in this world, neither in the world to come." I knew that it was very serious but I believe it means when the Holy Spirit is ridiculed and rejected because of unbelief. Mrs. Johnson was a strong believer but had not experienced some of the gifts of the Spirit and I knew that was the reason God had sent me – just to reassure her.

Leaning over to give her a hug, I said, "Oh, Mrs. Johnson, I do not know if that is unpardonable or not but I know that you will go to heaven and that Jesus loves you very much. Handing the pot of flowers to her, I added, "He even sent you flowers."

Isaiah 30:21 "Whether you turn to the right or to the left, your ears will hear a voice behind you, saying, 'This is the way; walk in it.

SEEK HIS WILL!

Eating a piece of fruit didn't seem so important that they should ask God about it, but Adam and Eve found out differently. It is so easy to make decisions without asking God what He wants you to do. Sometimes we think we know best and sometimes we think it is something so insignificant that God wouldn't care. But He does. Where you are concerned, He cares about everything.

"This Old House"

We were elated! We had just been given the opportunity to buy the small Texas farm that my husband's family had rented when he was growing up. It included one hundred and sixty acres of wheat, cotton and grazing land plus an old four-room house through which the wind whistled. It wasn't two bedrooms and a bath. It was four rooms and a path. When nature called, you went outside to an outhouse to visit her. The house wasn't old and quaint. It was old, ugly and in bad shape.

It had linoleum on the floor, faded wallpaper on the walls to hide the cracks, an old butane heater in the living room and nothing to give out heat in the bedrooms. The high ceilings were all smoked up; there were no closets anywhere, and rats often ran across the floors and sometimes even the beds. When I had visited as a teen-ager, it had been full of love and fun but now it just looked dismal and terribly inconvenient.

By that time, I was teaching, taking care of a husband and five children, holding too many jobs in the church and community and I was catching myself running even in my sleep. I really had no time for inconveniences like outdoor plumbing.

I remember, as I was driving down the road out of town and toward the farm, I started praying about the house. "Lord, I can do this and I will be grateful for it. If you want us to live in the old house, help me to do it without complaining. If you want us to build a new house, let Weldon decide that would be the best. Whatever your will is, I truly want it. Please take over."

When I got to the old place, Weldon walked out to the car and said, "I have arranged to sell some of the land to a builder who will tear this old house down and build us a new one. I think this is a good time rather than wait for five years as we had planned."

Six months later, we moved into a brand new four-bedroom, two-bath brick home with a living room, large den and kitchen. Five years down the road, the price of building had doubled. I learned again that the Lord wants only the best for us if we are willing to let him take control.

---

1 John 5:14 And this is the confidence that we have in him that, if we ask any thing according to his will, he hears us: 15 And if we know that he hears us, whatever we ask, we know that we have the petitions that we asked of him.

JUST DO IT!

Sometimes, when the voice is small, you really wonder if you are a little crazy. The Bible says that in the days of Samuel, "the word of the Lord was rare; there were not many visions." When God spoke to Samuel, Samuel thought it was Eli, the priest, and ran to him three times before Eli realized it was God speaking. If you aren't listening for His voice, it is sometimes hard to recognize.

"Radio Blip"

It was not always easy to do what I thought I heard God say to do. Once, on my way to go shopping in Wichita Falls, I heard on the radio about a Right to Life Conference that was being held at Luby's Cafeteria. Then I heard in my spirit, "Go there."

"Lord, is that really you? Are you sure?"

When I arrived, I stood in a line, only to be told, when I got to the front, that there were no tickets left. I turned to go, thinking, "I heard you wrong, I guess," when a man approached and said, "I can't stay so I won't need this ticket." The lady handed me the ticket, said, "I guess you get a free ticket." I went in and sat down at the back, at a table with four other women.

Suddenly, the Holy Spirit told me to turn to the woman on my right, which I did, and He spoke through me to her, "Don't be afraid of this move you are making, says the Lord. I will be with you." Then some other things were said that I don't remember. She started crying and said, "How did you know? I have been so afraid. I did not want to make this move." She went on to tell the rest of the women what had been happening. One of the other women, laughing, asked me, "Can you do that for me?"

John 10:27 "My sheep hear my voice, and I know them, and they follow me."

"CHRISTMAS RUSH"

One holiday season when my children seemed to be hurried, harried with gift-buying, decorating, parties and all stressed out, I thought, "Oh, how I wish I could give them a day just to rest and relax.

Father God quickly said to my spirit, "I did that!"

He did. He gave us a whole day and told us to honor it and keep it holy so that we could rest and spend time with Him.

I am sorry that the Sabbath day of rest is not observed anymore. Stores are opened, ballgames are played, lawns are mowed. Our children don't even realize that the Sabbath was meant to be a day of rest for them. On my day of rest, I love to relax with family, or when they are not around I like to paint, read, nap and pray. It is a day of rejuvenation for the week ahead.

Exodus 20:9,10 "Six days you shall labor and do all your work, but the seventh day is a Sabbath to the Lord your God. On it you shall not do any work."

GIVE YOUR DESIRES TO HIM!

When David was a little shepherd boy, he yearned to go with his big brothers to fight. But David had to stay out on those deserted hills, tending sheep, while his brothers got to go join the army. He spent his time out there worshipping God and talking to Him about his desires. Later, God gave David his desires and more. Who would have thought that the shepherd would become the king?

"Wanderlust"

I wanted to travel. I have always had a bad case of "wanderlust." Mother said that I inherited it from my Grandmother Sanders, who, the day she died, was planning a trip to Hawaii. My husband, however, never wanted to go farther than the local "Sweet Shop." Add to that his natural tendency to save money and we have a bit of a problem. I should have checked it out before I married him, but it didn't seem important then.

I would still have married him, but at least I would have known that my travel adventures were not in line with his ideas of the good life. He was a wonderful husband, father and provider. He would do anything for his family but he didn't want anything for himself. All he needed was a recliner, food at regular intervals and a television set for ball games and he was perfectly contented. I asked him one day, when he had watched football all day long, if he was going to be happy in Heaven without ballgames. He looked at me as if I had lost my mind and said, "What makes you think there won't be ballgames in Heaven?"

Since our ideas were definitely different, we had a few arguments, especially about traveling. I thought family vacations were important for the memories but also to show the children that there were other places in the world than the little Texas town in which we lived. We had never gone anywhere farther than Oklahoma City and Dallas, and those were for family events.

One night we had really gotten into a terrible argument and it had become loud and angry. I wanted a vacation. He didn't. He wasn't budging. He didn't want to travel and we didn't have the money and that was that! Of course, I knew that he could find money when he wanted to, like when he "found" money to build a swimming pool for the kids. I reminded him of this and a few other times when he "didn't have any money" but bought something expensive, "like the vacuum cleaner that I told you I did not want, but you bought it anyway!" He just stopped talking and went back to whatever sporting event was on television at the time.

I felt guilty about being so angry and wanting my way but that didn't stop me from stomping back to the bedroom and slamming the door. I fumed and fussed for a while. Then, I got down on my knees and said, "Lord, I don't want this fighting. I am not going to allow a desire of mine to create this kind of hostility in our marriage. If I never get to go anywhere ever, I am giving it to you. If you want me to travel or you don't want me to travel, I am leaving it up to you. If you want me to stay right here and never go past the Sweet Shop, it is going to be your call. You will have to do it because I am not going to say another word."

That was hard to do – to give up one of my dreams. But I rested easier that night and we made up before we went to bed. The next night, as we were enjoying a relaxing evening, Sandra, a good friend called. When I answered, she said, "Billie, A.J. just won a trip for two to Hawaii. You know how he hates to fly. Would you like to go with me?"

Would I? I couldn't believe it. How fast God answers when you let Him take over! After that, God arranged so many trips that I've lost track of them. I've gone to France, South Africa, Scotland, Ireland, England, Morocco, Ukraine, Moldova, Poland, Belarus, Israel, Italy, Greece, the Caribbean, Hawaii, Alaska, and Quebec, some several times. And, yes, once in a while, my husband even decided to go.

Psalm 37:4,5 "Delight yourself also in the Lord; and he shall give you the desires of your heart. 5 Commit your way unto the Lord; trust also in him; and he shall bring it to pass."

ASK HIM

When Nebuchadnezzar had a dream, everyone got involved or else heads were going to roll. Daniel knew what to do. He asked God and God not only told him what the dream was, but also what it meant. Whatever you need to know, God is always willing to give you the answer. You only have to ask and believe that He hears.

"Paradise Lost"

We were going on a vacation to paradise. I figured that anywhere we went outside of Burkburnett, Texas, was bound to be paradise. Weldon had the money for it in his billfold, (four hundred dollars and a check for another two hundred.) You couldn't get out of the county for that now, but back then, it was big bucks to us.

When we came home from a football game, he discovered that he didn't have his billfold. We looked everywhere, including the house, the barn, and the car. He and Ed, a friend, searched every room. We went back to the football field, afraid that he had dropped it there and someone might have picked it up. It was nowhere to be found and the grounds-keepers said that they had not seen it.

Finally, Weldon said, "We might as well face it. It's gone. I guess we won't get to go on that vacation after all." I might have thought that he had done it on purpose, knowing how he hated to go anywhere, but the look on his face showed me he was sick about losing the money. I prayed, "Lord, please show Weldon your faithfulness. Please help us find the billfold. Still, no billfold was anywhere to be found.

Weldon was sitting in his recliner, shaking his head. This was one of the few times that I had ever seen him upset because of losing something. Refusing to give up, I returned to the football stadium to look one more time. It just was not there.

I was driving back home when I thought, "I haven't asked the Lord where it is." So I asked Him to show me. Suddenly, in my mind a picture of the inside bottom of the built-in bedroom desk flashed before me. I went home, crawled under the desk, and there it was, under the edge and so much the same color of the desk that it was not visible anywhere but directly underneath it.

We did get to go on vacation and believe me, all the way to Paradise, (the Ozark Mountains,) I was praising the Lord. Weldon was just looking forward to getting back home.

James 1:5 "If any of you lack wisdom, let him ask of God, that gives to all men liberally, and without reproach; and it shall be given to him.

OBEY EVEN WHEN IT'S COSTLY!

Abraham finally had the son that God had promised him and God said, "Go sacrifice your son as a burnt offering. Abraham's obedience was the most amazing thing I have ever seen until Jesus obeyed the Father and sacrificed himself to give us eternal life.

"One Thousand Dollar Give-Away"

The Lord had answered another prayer. I had asked for an exercise program and one was started at the church. It was hard interrupting the day, but it was fun and I was enjoying the women, young and old, who came.

We all circled around and prayed afterward. One woman's prayer, about a woman she knew who was dying, penetrated my heart and I felt like I was supposed to do something about it, so I asked for more information, thinking I could pray more effectively if I knew the whole story.

Julia told me that her friend had something wrong with her that would kill her in a short time if she did not have an operation. She said that, because of all of her medical bills, the doctors and hospital would not perform the operation unless she came up with a thousand dollars.

I thought, "That can't be true. No one would let someone die if they didn't have the money to pay."

Julia assured me that it was true and that the woman had gone everywhere to borrow it but her credit was so bad that no one would loan it to her. Her family and friends would have given her the money but none of them had it.

I went home and started praying for Francis to get the thousand dollars that she needed and that the operation would be performed soon enough to save her life. Wouldn't you know, the Lord, in the middle of one of my prayers, said, "You give it to her."

"What?" I don't have a thousand dollars!"

"You have that thousand dollars that you have been saving in the bank."

"But I was trying to start saving in case we needed it for an emergency."

"This is an emergency."

"Are you sure this is what you want me to do. This could be a fake request. She might be one of those people who ...... okay, Lord, if you say so."

That night I called Francis and told her to bring me the information about the doctor and I would write a check to him for the thousand dollars. I gave her my mother's address so that she would not have to find our home in the country.

The next day, she came to the front door of my mother's house and when I answered the door, I was shocked to see a young woman who looked like she had just come out of a concentration camp, she was so thin. Her eyes were large circles on top of black shadows. I was amazed that she could still stand.

She sat on one of the chairs on the porch as I made out the check to the doctor and through tears, she kept saying, "Thank you."

Through her friend, Julia, I heard that she had come through the operation fine but I didn't hear from her for a couple of months. When she did come to thank me again, I didn't recognize her. Her face and figure were much fuller and her eyes were sparkling.

Now, I didn't put this story in to tell you how great I was but to tell you how faithful our heavenly Father is. You see, a few months after I had given a stranger a thousand dollars, I received an inheritance that I never expected. Twenty-one thousand dollars! You truly cannot out-give God.

Luke 6:38 "Give, and it will be given to you. A good measure, pressed down, shaken together and running over, will be poured into your lap. For with the measure you use, it will be measured to you."

MAKE OBEDIENCE YOUR PRIORITY

Many opportunities are missed when you do not obey the Lord's voice immediately or you argue with Him. Think "Jonah." He ended up preaching in Ninevah but he went through a dark night in a fish's belly first. Being regurgitated upon the rocks wouldn't have been too pleasant either.

"Church on the Rock"

A sister church in our small town was having a ladies' retreat and had asked me to be one of the speakers. I was delighted to hear that some ladies from large churches in Dallas were going to be the main speakers. I had fun and everyone enjoyed themselves, laughing at some of the stories I told about my crazy family.

At the end of the day, the speakers from a Dallas church called Church on the Rock, asked if I would come and sign up for their speakers' bureau. I was excited because that was something that I would have loved.

But I kept putting it off. I had a husband, his mother, who lived with us, five children and eleven grandchildren who lived on the same road, as well as my own parents and a job as a curriculum director. Living in one town for over forty years and working in the church allows you to stay very involved and it pretty well kept every week filled to the max. It seemed like there was always something else to finish before I felt like I could go. I had good excuses.

One day, at church, I thought that Jesus was telling me that He wanted me to go to Church on the Rock and sign up for that speakers' bureau. I said, "Lord, this may be just my own thoughts wanting my own desire so if it is really you speaking, I need you to tell me for sure that you want me to go." As we stood up to sing, a young man sitting beside me whom I had never seen in our church before, turned to me and asked, "Have you ever been to Church on the Rock?"

With my mouth hanging open, I could only shake my head. He pointed a finger at me and said, "You ought to go."

I regret to say that even when you know it is God's voice, you can choose to be disobedient. I procrastinated until it was too late and it is one of my largest regrets, knowing that I missed God's plan and a wonderful opportunity. I paid dearly for my disobedience. I became a school principal.

---

1 Samuel 15:22 "To obey is better than sacrifice."

YOU DON'T HAVE TO LIKE IT!

When Joseph was sold as a slave in Egypt and was later thrown into prison, he was probably wondering, "What did I do to deserve this? This prison is not where I should be. This cannot be God's plan for my life. I must have heard wrong." God meant it all for good, but at the time, it was the pits!

"I HATE IT!"

I was being given the opportunity to leave the job I loved as curriculum director and take the principal's job. I didn't want it. The superintendent didn't want me to take it, but it was my decision, he said. My family didn't think I should. But I felt that God was telling me to do it.

I spent the week-end at our lake cabin, praying for direction. I was really praying that God would not want me to leave what I loved doing to go into the worst school in the district as a principal. I knew I was just trying to get God to change His mind. He didn't, so I told the superintendent that I would take the job. And a job it was!

My first day of school, I had thirteen discipline referrals, five upset parents, a giant of a boy who was running the halls, five gang members, (teachers who were fighting against me from the beginning,) and only one secretary to run interference. I hated it!

Those were five of the worst years of my life but they were also some of my best gifts. Every morning, at five o'clock, I woke up to plead with God to carry me and He did. He even gifted me with the words and music for forty songs, although I had no musical background. He did it all during those five years of battling teachers, parents, and the administration to try to make a better school for a part of the town that had the lowest income families.

We promoted the school by trying many innovative ideas: "Fantastic Fridays," in which business people and artists taught classes, "Enrichment periods," where children were exposed to art, music, drama, and Spanish, and musical assemblies that made "stars" out of all children. It almost killed some of my friends and me. But the rewards were great! The children and most of the teachers loved the school.

One of my favorite memories is walking down the hall and listening to all of the children singing "The Star Spangled Banner" and Lee Greenwood's "I'm Proud to be an American." By that time, we had taken discipline referrals from 1700 my first year to a small folder that held the names of twenty-one students. One of the kids told his teacher that he wanted to be a principal when he grew up because, "All she does is walk the halls and hug kids."

---

2 Corinthians 4:17 "For our light and momentary troubles are achieving for us an eternal glory that far outweighs them all."

LESSON THIRTEEN

EXPECT AN ANSWER!

When the church was praying for Peter to get out of prison, they were surprised when an angel delivered him right to their doorstep. They almost didn't open the door for him. They were praying but not expecting an answer.

"Sugar Blues"

I had been to three medical centers in three different cities and still no one had found the reason that my hands and fingers were hurting. Now, it was moving up my arms and the pain kept me awake all night. I was always tired and cranky and would cry at the drop of a wrong word from anyone. My mother thought for sure I had cancer. My husband thought it was my job getting to me. My children thought someone had exchanged their mother for the "wicked witch of the west." I couldn't think at all.

After coming home from the last medical center, I was so discouraged that I just fell on my face and said. "Please, God, help me." The next day, a friend called and asked if I would go with her to a weight reduction meeting called "Overeaters Anonymous." The only thing they seemed to stress was to remove sugar and white flour from your diet. My friend even brought me some whole wheat bread so that I could start immediately.

Three weeks later, I was fifteen pounds lighter and my pain was gone. But any time that I ate sugar, my hands started hurting and I couldn't sleep.

That should have been enough motivation for anyone to kick the sugar habit but no, I was a sweet-a-holic. Sugar was my main reward and relaxer. You know what I mean. I ate sweets to make me feel better if something had gone wrong and to celebrate if something had gone right. Having little time to relax, I substituted sweets for resting and I could tell myself that "life is good" if I had that sugary dessert to gobble on. There was even a time that I got up in the middle of the night and made an apple pie because I had to have something sweet.

Knowing that sugar was killing me should have made me eliminate it easily, but I couldn't make myself stop eating it. One day before Thanksgiving, I was desperate. I had brought home chocolate do-nuts and chocolate chip cookies that were left-over from a celebration at school. (That is the way a lot of us celebrate.) I got down on my knees in my dining room and prayed for thirty or forty minutes begging God to please deliver me from my addiction to sugar. Then I got up and started eating a do-nut as I started cooking pies for Thanksgiving.

The phone rang and I reached for it, taking the last bite and swallowing quickly. Debbie, an acquaintance who has become a dear friend, was on the other end of the line and said, "Will you promise not to laugh at me if I tell you something that I think God told me to tell you?"

"Of course I won't laugh," I replied, thinking how wonderful to hear something from God.

She said with a little hesitation in her voice, "Well, for about thirty or forty minutes, I have been arguing with God because I felt He wanted me to call you and tell you something but it doesn't make any sense and I don't want you to laugh. I think God wanted me to call and say one word to you. Sugar! Does He want us to go out and buy a lot of sugar or what?"

I roared with laughter. I couldn't help it.

She said, "You promised you would not laugh. I guess I was wrong."

"No, no. Don't hang up. You were right. But I am laughing because you just got in on one of the fastest answers to prayer that I've ever had! Then I told her about the prayer and assured her that she had done a wonderful thing in being so obedient. Her obedience would change my life.

It has been many years now and if I fall, it is usually from not reading all of the ingredients. Was it easy to quit sugar? No, it was still difficult but knowing that God cares and is listening made it so much easier.

Isaiah 65:24 "Before they call, I will answer; while they are still speaking I will hear."

LESSON FOURTEEN

DOUBT YOUR DOUBTS!

When Jesus was resurrected, his disciples could not believe it, until he walked through the wall and showed them his hands and his side. How do you imagine they felt, having deserted Him in the Garden of Gethsemane? Like we do, sometimes?

"Covered With His Righteousness"

Many times, I feel too dirty to come before the Lord.

I'll never forget a time when I was praying for a man in agony with a sickness the doctors could not diagnose. One night, in desperation, his wife, a friend of mine, called everyone she knew who might pray for him. Her husband had been sick for so long with so many diseases that I didn't know how he could stand it. She asked me to pray for him because he was suffering with terrible constant itching and so much pain that he didn't want to live.

When I hung up, I immediately got to my knees and started praying. I suddenly saw myself in God's throne room, dirty and in filthy ragged clothes. The devil appeared and whispered in my ear, "You should not be here. You are too ugly and dirty,"

I agreed and started to retreat. Humiliated, I wanted to leave as quickly as possible. But, just then, Jesus walked down from the left side of the throne. (My first thought was, "He's supposed to be on the right hand of the Father," and then I realized that my left side was God's right side.) Jesus stepped over to me, wrapped himself around me, covering me with His robe of righteousness, and said, "Now, let's go to the Father."

The next morning at 6:45 a.m., my friend called to tell me what had happened. She said her husband had taken pain medicine and gone to bed about 11:00. He woke up in terrible pain at 12:00, but could have no more medicine for two hours. He went to lay on the recliner so that he wouldn't disturb her. She checked on him twice. Once his head was hanging off the recliner but she didn't want to disturb him since it looked like he was finally resting. The next time he was snoring.

When the alarm went off at 5:00, he came in and told her that he had experienced something really strange.

After he had moved to the recliner, he said that he was in terrible pain for a long time and then, suddenly, he was floating above his body and was looking down at himself in the chair. He didn't know how long he was hovering there but he felt no pain. Then suddenly he was back in his body, and still no pain. He slept the rest of the night and for months after that was completely free of pain.

I know that many people were praying for him and that my prayers were not the only ones that made a difference, but that night made a difference for me as I realized that because we are covered in Jesus' righteousness, God hears our prayers.

This is another song that the Lord gave me.

I'm not the same,
I'm not the same,
The devil will deny the fact,
But I'm not the same.

The robe of righteousness He gave me,
When I asked the Lord to save me,
Made the change,
And now I'm not the same.

Isaiah 61:10 "I delight greatly in the Lord; my soul rejoices in my God. For he has clothed me with garments of salvation and arrayed me in a robe of his righteousness…"

PRAISE BRINGS THE ANSWER!

When King Jehoshaphat was told about a vast army coming against the people of Judah, he appointed men to go before the army, singing and praising the Lord. Then the Lord set ambushes and miraculously defeated their enemies.

"A Surprise Trip to Florida"

It was a wonderful surprise – four women, passionate about Jesus, a trip through the south, a free condo, and the whitest beach in Florida! We didn't even know each other when we started but the Lord had arranged this trip to keep me from going ballistic in a house that had become a little crowded. My mother-in-law lived with us and because of Parkinson's disease and the medicine she took, started experiencing horrible hallucinations. Along with that, my oldest daughter, her husband and their three children, four, three, and a baby, had moved in while their house was being remodeled. I did not realize that I was hanging so close to the edge but the Lord did and so he arranged a delightful trip with three wonderful Christian ladies and he ordered every mile of it.

Pat, a friend of mine had been asked by Jan, a friend of hers to bring someone with her on a vacation to her condo in Florida for a couple of weeks. She was bringing another friend, Linda, and that would make a nice foursome. I was only too happy to oblige. So, getting the go-ahead from my husband, we started out.

Destin was our destination but the whole trip through the beautiful south was fabulous. We stayed in a real southern mansion. We toured many plantations because we "just happened" to be in the towns when they were having their plantation tours. We found the quaintest little restaurants that served the best fresh fish you could imagine. The best part of all was that we all were Christians so we sang and praised the Lord all the way.

Our vacation lasted longer than we had hoped because of waiting for another friend to come from Miami to ride home with us. We didn't mind a bit. The only stress we had been under was when we burned a pot of beans and the smoke alarm went off. Every time we thought about leaving, I would roll up in a fetal position and start sucking my thumb.

After ten days, Linda's husband called and asked when we were returning. She told him that we were being held hostage. Our husbands back at home went to eat together and, when the waitress asked them, "Do your wives know where you are?" they replied, "No, and we don't know where they are either." But finally, when everyone started saying nice things about their husbands, I told them, "It must be time to go home."

So all we needed to start the trip back to Texas was the friend from Miami. Later, we discovered she had a nervous break-down and was going back and forth on the highways, not able to find her way. We began to worry about her when she still had not arrived two days after she had started.

We waited and waited and at six o'clock one evening, we finally decided it was time to pray. As we were praying, I was impressed that we should just start praising the Lord, and that is what we did. As soon as we started singing praises, the telephone rang and it was the friend in a phone booth around the corner.

I will forever praise Him for that wonderful vacation in Florida and will remember that praise breaks through when nothing else can.

Philippians 4:6 "Do not be anxious about anything, but in every situation, by prayer and supplication, with thanksgiving, let your request be made known unto God, and the peace of God, which passes all understanding, will keep your hearts and minds in Christ Jesus."

INVITE HIM IN!

When Zaccheus, the small-statured tax-collector, was told," I'm going to your house today," he was excited and honored that Jesus would want to go home with him. Shouldn't we be honored that Jesus wants to spend time with us?

" Knocking At The Door "

I looked at the clock. Two o'clock in the morning! Who would be knocking on the door at two in the morning? It must be an emergency. I jumped out of bed, grabbing a housecoat, flipped on the lights inside and out, opened the door. No one was there. Stepping out on the porch, I looked around to see who had knocked. Deciding that it was probably some kids at a slumber party playing tricks, I went back to bed and to sleep.

A few nights later, it happened again. If it was my grandchildren who lived next door, I was going to get them. But, when I mentioned it, no one knew what I was talking about. In fact, they were concerned that I might not be safe and urged me to keep my door locked and call them.

The knocking happened so often that I sometimes would just think, "Another prankster," and turn over and go back to sleep. But then my sister-in-law and I went to the Pocono Mountains in Pennsylvania for a week's vacation. We had a two-story condo and we were sound asleep one night when someone started knocking on the door. I tried to wake Barb but I couldn't rouse her. It was a little scary going down stairs, wondering with every step, "Who could need us in the middle of the night?" I asked at the door, "Who's there?"

Leaving the inside light off, I turned on the porch light and peered out through the curtains. No one was there. I did not open the door but went back to bed, thinking, "What is going on here. This knocking on the door is getting really strange."

Back home in Texas, when the knocks came again, I finally asked, "Lord Jesus, what is going on?"

I guess He had been waiting for me to ask because I heard in my spirit the verse from Revelation 3:20, "I stand at the door and knock, whoever hears my voice and opens to me, I will come in and sup with him and he with me."

"Oh, Lord, I know that scripture but I thought you were in. I didn't mean to leave you out."

"Do you remember the song that I gave you about not dying?" He asked.

"Of course, Lord."

"I shall not die before I have seen my Savior,
I shall not die before I have seen my Lord,
I shall not die before I have seen Messiah,
For He is now, even now, He is at the door.

Open the door and live with me forever,
Open the door and see what I have in store,
Open the door, I want you with me forever,
For I am here, even now, I am at the door."

When I think of that "Here I am," I cannot keep from remembering one of my grandsons, who was three or four at the time, coming to see us from Dallas. He would come out the back gate, looking for us in the garden or the pasture, with his arms open wide and a grin on his face, "Memaw, Grandad, here I am."

I believe it is that kind of joy which Jesus is bestowing on us when He says, "Dear One, here I am! Open the door."

The knocking sometimes is so insistent that I still get up to answer the door, but then I go back to bed and I ask the Lord to forgive me for keeping Him on the outside again. I had always thought that the scripture about standing at the door and knocking was inviting unsaved people to be saved. Finally, I realized that the warning was for the Laodocean Church, the lukewarm church in the book of Revelation. Jesus wasn't speaking to people who weren't saved; He was speaking to church members who were shutting Him out of their lives.

1 John 3:1 "See what great love the Father has lavished on us, that we should be called children of God!"

"SACRIFICE?"

Once, when I was driving home, just as I turned under the overpass, the Lord spoke to my spirit, showing me an altar and said, "Lay yourself down on my altar." I thought, "That is a big order. I don't know if I can do that, Lord, to give up everything to you.....to yield my whole being, to sacrifice my all on that altar." But, then I realized that He had always been my everything and he had sacrificed himself for me. So, in my mind's eye, I lay down on the altar. Then I saw the altar moving with me in it. At just that moment, I realized that the altar was really God's hands and as I lay in His hands, he was moving me closer to himself.

REMEMBER WHO HE IS!

When Jesus said that He was the Rock, He meant it. He was the rock that David cast to bring down a giant. He was the rock from which water poured for the Israelites in the desert. He is the rock upon which His church is built. Jesus, the Lord himself, is the Rock eternal.

"MY ROCK WAS ON A MOUNTAIN IN SCOTLAND."

It was a little scary, taking four teen-agers who were not mine on a trip to the British Isles. Our tour director's daughter had been involved in a serious accident which made it impossible for her to go on the trip. But one of the mothers was also going and I asked the Lord to take over.

Everything had gone really well and I was falling in love with the kids. We had seen beautiful Ireland and kissed the "blarney stone." We had toured castles in Scotland in freezing rain and were about to leave Scotland to go to London when we stopped at a small mountain peak. Of course the kids wanted to climb up a little way and I followed them in heels. That was not really smart. I was stumbling up the mountain and one of the kids called, "Billie, will you take a picture of us?"

I looked up, stumbled and suddenly I was falling over the edge of the mountain.

Thankfully a large rock stopped my fall. Had it not been for that rock being at that exact spot, I would have fallen down the mountain. I said, "Thank you, Lord, that that rock was right there to catch me."

When I got back home, I was looking back at the prayer journal that I had written the day before our trip. The scriptures I had written were: "He is my Rock." "Ps. 62:5 and "My soul, wait only upon God; for my hope is only from him. He only is my rock and my salvation."

That was no coincidence. He gave me those scriptures and He gave me that rock.

LESSON EIGHTEEN

TRUST HIM!

I have an affinity for Peter. He was so tempestuous. He was always jumping into things, making promises, climbing out of boats, wanting to be with Jesus. So what if he messed up a little?

"Get Out Of The Boat"

"You can't die! I love you!" I was screaming this to my husband as my daughter and I, and later, the EMT's, tried to revive him from a massive heart attack. Knowing that he had heart trouble had not prepared me for the final event. The next five months were a blur in which I ate, slept, and stared at the walls, unless my children and grandchildren were there. I tried to act as normal as possible when they were around. My tears and hysterics I saved for the times when I was alone.

Five months after we buried Weldon., I asked the Lord, "What now? What do you have for me to do now? Whatever you want, I will do as long as you are with me." That same night, at the church that I've attended most of my life, a missionary spoke. He said, "We need some people to fill out a team that we are taking to Russia on a mission trip. We will conduct English schools and tell people about Jesus and His love."

I was interested. I had retired from education, having taught for twenty-three years. Thinking that perhaps sometime in the future I might want to do something like that, I walked over to the people who were answering questions and asked, "What would I need to do to get ready for a trip like that?"

One of the ladies asked me, "Do you have a passport?"

I said, "Yes."

Three weeks later, I had been trained and was on a flight to Ukraine with a group of fifteen people whom I didn't know, going to a place where I had never been, to do something I had never done. The apostle, Peter, had nothing on me. I had truly stepped out of the boat.

It was culture shock for sure. We dealt with "squatty potties", the language barrier, and suspicious Ukrainians. It took a week for them to begin to trust us. They still couldn't figure out why a group of Americans would use their own money to come to teach them English and tell them about Jesus. But by the second week, we all fell in love with each other. One of the songs that we sang and which had to be my personal theme song for that trip was, "I Will Never Be the Same Again."

Jeremiah 29:11 "For I know the plans I have for you, declares the Lord, plans to prosper you and not to harm you, plans to give you hope and a future.

DO NOT BE AFRAID!

Those three young Hebrew men who refused to bow down to Nebuchadnezzar's golden statue didn't seem to be afraid but the picture in their mind of that burning furnace had to have terrified them. Or maybe not.

"Kidnapped By Gypsies"

We stayed in the apartments with Ukrainians who spoke no English but were the most gracious and hospitable of hosts. They shared their small rooms and food with us. They also taught us to watch out for pick-pockets, especially Gypsy children who were trained to steal and warned us that Gypsies had even kidnapped people.

This really did not make much of an impression on me until the fourth day of class when a beautiful lady dressed in flowing rainbows of color stopped me and started talking to me in Russian. I knew no Russian but I invited her to come into the classes. She always shook her head. We gestured and tried to talk with hands and arms, smiling and laughing with each other. She came every day after that, never going into the classes, but always spending time trying to communicate with me.

Several times she would motion for me to go with her across the street to a café for coffee but we were not allowed to leave the church grounds with anyone other than our hosts and the American team. She kept making gestures with her hands and arms more insistently every day. On the last day of the school, I was surprised to see her on the third floor of the church.

Grabbing my hand, she dragged me down the three flights of stairs and outside where three men sat in a rusty, rattle-trap of a car. One of the men got out and she pushed me into the back seat, telling him to get in beside me. She then grabbed another Ukrainian girl, pushed her into the front seat, and got in beside her. Slamming the door and motioning to the driver, we were off, amid loud protests from me in the back seat. She and the others laughed merrily and made the same arm gestures that she had made to me each day.

The car was amazingly fast to be so old and I thought, "I've been kidnapped by Gypsies and I will never see my family again." As they kept driving and I kept thinking what they might do to me, I began to pray, "Please, Lord Jesus, no one knows where I am except you. Help me."

Isaiah 41:10 came to my mind: "Fear not; for I am with you; be not dismayed' for I am your God: I will strengthen you; yes, I will help you; yes, I will uphold you with the right hand of my righteousness." Then came the peace that passes all understanding. Suddenly I was not afraid. "Lord, you have watched over me my entire life and I know you will never leave me."

We continued driving for what seemed like hours but was probably only twenty or thirty minutes, when we arrived at a forested area. As they pulled me out of the car, I thought about all of the people who disappear into forests and are never heard from again. We walked down dirt footpaths, ever deeper into the gloomy woods of huge old trees, wild shrubs and undergrowth.

A few minutes of persuasive nudging from them and we were in a clearing. The scene in front of me was something I will never forget. It was unlike anything I had ever seen before. It reminded me of old Russian folktales. There, before me, was a beautiful crystal lake and floating on its still surface were dozens of amazing pure white swans!

That was what the gestures were all about, what this kidnapping was all about. They liked me and they didn't want me to leave their city without experiencing the spectacular sight of the swans on that lake. I cried and hugged them, said "spaseeba" over and over again. They laughed like small children.

Then they took me back to the church. We hugged good-bye and I went into the church to join the rest of the team. They were singing my theme song. This time I sang it with a little Russian accent, "I VILL never be the same again."

ASK FOR A FLEECE!

When God told Gideon that He was going to use him to save Israel, Gideon had a hard time believing it, so he placed a wool fleece on the ground and asked God to put dew on the fleece while the ground remained dry. And that is what happened. He still wasn't sure that He was hearing God correctly, that it wasn't his imagination, so he asked God to make the fleece dry and the ground wet. And He did.

That is why I am not hesitant to throw out a fleece when I'm not certain that it is God speaking. I need to be sure it is not my own crazy thoughts.

"Sell My House?"

I cannot do this! Nothing works! How do I take care of this without Weldon? My house was a twenty-five year old, ranch-style brick home on a sixty-acre farm two miles outside of town and I loved it. But since my husband's death, it seemed as if everything was breaking down at the same time. (Since then, I have discovered this often happens when spouses die.)

My house was stretched out with four bedrooms off of a long hall, a large den, and a small living room that I had turned into a dining room because we always needed more tables for our brood. With five children, their spouses, ten grandchildren, their many friends and all of our in-laws, we needed plenty of table space for our weekly get-togethers to celebrate birthdays, holidays or any other excuse. The long hall was perfect for running, jumping for the ceiling or as a runway for bowling.

We had a formal table in the dining room, a round table that could be extended into a long one in the den, a long trestle table in the kitchen and another round one in the sun room.

I loved that sun room. I had always wanted one and Weldon, who was given a whole trailer-full of windows and always loved using anything he got for free, built it for me. Not only did I get a sun room but he decided we should have a cellar underneath it. All the visiting kids enjoyed going up and down in that cellar. It was great!

I also had the nicest view of some sloping wheat fields and, across the Red River, the hills of Oklahoma. In back of the house was a covered back porch and a pathway to the swimming pool with a cabana that the grandkids thought was excellent to use for jumping into the pool when parents were not around. The kids and I would climb up on the cabana at night with our blankets, pillows and snacks and watch the stars. The back yard wasn't fancy, just a lot of fun.

The sidewalk also led to the mother-in-law apartment where my husband's mother had lived for the last twenty years of her life. The rest of my domain included a triple garage that usually had everything stored in it except cars, a big metal barn and a low red barn, which was on its last legs but was still used as hay storage.

We had great celebrations, birthdays, graduation parties, baby showers, and holidays. On Christmas, every room was decorated with bears, toys, garlands and trees. Our other families came up from Fort Worth to celebrate with us. They even endured, with laughter, our kids' programs and performances.

Then there was the wonderful 4th of July. We never knew how many people were here for that celebration. I introduced myself as they came in and out, helping themselves to the home-made ice cream, the hot dogs, the hamburgers and the watermelon. I loved the big old front porch where we all sat to watch fireworks. We could see our own display, our neighbors, the town's, and some over in Oklahoma. Our yard was full of blankets, lawn chairs and kids.

For our den, I had just invested in a huge purple couch with a large French chair and ottoman in a matching design. Several years before I had bought a French provincial table with rush seats. My husband never quite got over my buying that. But it sat nicely in front of our wide window seat which had newly installed white wooden shutters.

I had completely remodeled my kitchen with ceramic tile, new stainless steel appliances, and faux brick walls. After white-washing the cabinets, and with my trestle table and old cupboard, (which Weldon had found for me,) I had the French provincial kitchen I had always wanted.

Then the Lord said, "Sell it."

"What? That's my home. That's where all of my children have grown up. That has too many wonderful memories."

Two weeks before that, when I couldn't get the weed-eater to work and the lawn-mower wouldn't start and the pool had turned green for the fourth time, I had taken an axe, gone into the sunroom and chopped down all of the spindles that protected the area around the cellar door. No reason, just a moment of insanity.

But I wasn't that mad at my house. I certainly didn't want to sell it. I loved that old house, from the hole in the bathroom window through which Weldon had shot a coyote, to the wide-open pastures, to the problematic swimming pool. As soon as it got warm enough to swim, our pool was the favorite water hole of our kids, their kids and all of their friends. The adults would gather, lather, lay out and laugh at the kids and each other. Food and fun were served non-stop.

No, I could not sell my home. "Sorry, Lord, it is a lot of work and my kids are going to have to help but I could not sell it. Nope. No way. Not a chance. Pretty sure it's not you speaking. You wouldn't ask me to do that. I've lost Weldon. You wouldn't ask me to give up my home, my memories."

"You will take your memories with you."

"Okay, Lord, if this is really you, then let someone come and offer me this amount of money without my even mentioning it to anyone."

The next week, a realtor came to my door and asked if a couple could see my house. She said, "I know you don't have any thought of selling it, but this couple would really like to see it. Would you mind?"

You guessed it. They wanted to buy. I ended up with exactly the amount of money I had told the Lord I wanted. I had an estate sale, moved the remainder of my stuff into a storage pod, and moved out of the house the night before I left on another mission trip to Russia. I had no idea where I would live when I came back. But I kept telling the Lord all the time I was gone, "Lord, you know where you want me to live. It is all up to you."

The kids had built a pretty little house on the far end of our farm and had sold it quickly. However, for some strange reason, the couple's loan was cancelled and when I got back to Texas, I was suddenly moving into that brand new house.

Romans 8:28 "And we know that all things work together for good to them that love God, to them who are the called according to his purpose."

DON'T DISCOUNT IT JUST BECAUSE IT DOESN'T MAKE SENSE

I'm saying, "If it makes any sense at all, it probably isn't God." I have a lot of scripture to back that up. When God told Noah, "Noah, build a boat." I'll bet Noah thought, "There's no water, Lord; a boat won't float. But the reason that Noah could spend a hundred years building a boat is because he was like his great grandfather, Enoch, who walked with God. Now, if you are walking and talking with God, you can hear him better.

So Noah built a boat that would carry the equivalent of 522 railroad cars full of animals and God directed all of the animals to get in. (Someone has speculated that the animals were babies and that is how so many could live in that space. I just figure God can do whatever He wants to do, so I don't have to speculate.) Then he told Noah and his family to get in. God closed the door. He had to because Noah would not have been able to resist helping people escape the flood, especially family. But God took care of Noah's family. If you add up the ages, you will find that Noah's father, Lamech, and his grandfather, Methusaleh, both died right before the flood.

Then there was Joseph who started out thinking God must have some really big plans for him and ended up in a prison in Egypt. He had to have been scratching his head, thinking, "This makes no sense at all. Why am I here?" But God used him to save his family, Egypt, and a large part of Canaan from famine.

The Israelites didn't think it made any sense for God to bring them out into the wilderness only to be cornered between the Egyptian army and the Red Sea. But Moses told them to trust God and see that salvation would come from the Lord. (He had tried to do it his way when he killed an Egyptian years before and he knew it was only God who could save.)

Joshua had to think, "This is crazy," when God told him to have everybody walk around the city of Jericho six days and on the seventh, blow horns and shout. But the walls fell down.

Gideon was certainly not sure of himself when God told him to fight the Midianites and the Amelekites, who were pitched in the Valley of Jezreel. There were so many, they couldn't be counted and Gideon had only 22,000, which God said were too many. So when he only had 300, God said, "That's more like it. Now no one can fail to see that it is I who delivers. And just so there is no doubt about that, you're going to go out with only trumpets and pitchers with lamps in them." Talk about faith! As you know, God and Gideon's three hundred, won.

What about David? It was strange that God didn't want the oldest, the strongest, the tallest to be anointed king. He looked out in the desert and saw a little shepherd boy singing praises to Him and said,

"That's him." "That's my choice for king."

Then God put David in the right place at the right time to kill a GIANT? With a slingshot! How crazy is that? It made no sense!

It didn't make any sense for God to come to earth, to be born in the worst surroundings, to live a vagabond life, and to die the cruelest of deaths so that he could save mankind. I don't understand it, cannot comprehend it, and only by the Holy Spirit can I accept it. God, in Christ, came to save sinners.

Have you noticed that most of the heroes of the Bible had to come out of a wilderness, a prison, or captivity of some kind before God could use them?

Moses was in the wilderness and God called.

Noah was in the middle of a violent, evil civilization and God called.

Joseph was in a prison cell and God called.

Gideon was hiding in a threshing floor and God called.

Joshua had been trudging around the wilderness for forty years and God called.

Have you ever felt that you were in a wilderness just waiting for God to do something with you? Have you ever felt that you have wasted much of your life waiting?

I have often felt that way even though I have worked hard and run fast.

Sometimes I think, "God, if you really wanted to use me, you would move me out of here, give me a task to accomplish that would be important in your work.

He told me to go to college. WITH FOUR KIDS? He carried me all the way.

He told me to teach school. WITH FIVE KIDS? I thought perhaps it was my mission field.

He told me to become a counselor. WITH FIVE KIDS, A HUSBAND AND AN ELDERLY MOTHER IN LAW? I wanted to build an orphanage and take the children home with me.

He told me to become a principal. WITH FIVE KIDS, A HUSBAND, A MOTHER IN LAW, AND ELEVEN GRANDCHILDREN? I didn't like it. I hated it! But He took me through it with songs. I knew I was hearing from Him.

My husband got sick and slowly started going blind. God told me to retire early and take care of my husband, mother in law, and eleven grandchildren.

My husband died. "Why, Lord? I needed him. We needed him." God didn't tell me.

He told me to go with a mission team to Russia. TO RUSSIA? I DON'T KNOW THE LANGUAGE. I DON'T KNOW THE PEOPLE. I DON'T HAVE THE MONEY!

It made no sense at all.

He told me to sell my house.

I LOVED MY HOUSE!

Are you in the wilderness, wondering, "Why am I here?" Are you thinking, "Why is God allowing what is happening in my life, in my family, in our country?" If it doesn't make any sense at all, get ready and praise God, because you can believe that He is going to do something that only he can do.

Proverbs 3:5,6 "Trust in the Lord with all your heart and lean not on your own understanding. In all your ways, acknowledge Him and He shall direct your paths."

PRAISE THE LORD ANYWAY!

I love the story about Paul and Silas, chained down in a prison dungeon, singing songs of praise to God. It was such powerful praise that a great earthquake shook the foundations of the prison; all the doors were opened, and the chains fell off of the prisoners.

"Fire, Fire Everywhere!"

It was only the beginning of a long, hot summer in which much of Texas would dry up and burn up. The heat and high winds were already compelling us to stay inside our air conditioned homes where we could breathe.

Some of my children and grandchildren were visiting me when suddenly, there was a pounding on the front door and a policeman shouted. "Evacuate immediately! A fire is blazing across the wheat field and it is almost here!"

Everyone moved quickly to their cars. My youngest daughter, Jennifer, said, "My pictures." We had been going through some of them for graduation videos. We stuffed them into my car, without even thinking of my own pictures, and I said, "I'll meet you at your house." She was the only one of our family besides my mother who lived in town. Four of my children live on this road, my son, Bob, and three of my daughters and their families.

I turned at the corner and one of our friends said, "Meems, Bob is trying to hose down your house and trying to get Lisa's dog out of her house." When I pulled out my cell phone to tell him to get out of there, it was dead, of course, so I just watched and prayed as the fire went toward our houses. I prayed that the blood of Jesus would cover them and I then started praising the Lord and praying for the firemen. When it looked like all of our houses were gone, (the smoke was covering everything from my house on down,) I figured I'd better go tell my mother that we were safe. I told her and her neighbor, Ed, that it looked like all of our houses were gone. He said, "Let's pray" and we did.

"I'd better go let Jennifer know where I am," I said as I started out the door. "We will probably divide between your house and hers to sleep tonight."

As I turned on Jennifer's street, I could get no farther than the middle of the street. There was a fire at the other end! I got out and started running, thinking, "That looks like Jennifer's block. That's Jennifer's house! That couldn't be."

It was her house! The garage had started burning and it was going all through the house. No one was there when the fire started because Austin, her son, had gone looking for me and Jen had gone looking for him.

How strange is that? Our houses are burning on the north side of town and her house is burning on the south side. Janet, another daughter who was watching, drily pointed at me and said, "It looks to me like someone is not living right." I laughed. Something weird was definitely happening. But I was praising the Lord. In spite of all of our houses being gone, everyone was safe.

Then, we were told that our homes had been saved. The fire had come right to the front doors and stopped. The firemen said that it was a miracle that it was put out just there. But Jen's was a total loss. And it was her birthday!

I wonder if perhaps, as we were praying for the houses on one side, the devil was attacking our back side. I've noticed that he does that often.

"Lord," I said later, "I have been praying for the wind and fire but I meant the wind and fire of the Holy Spirit. I really didn't mean physical wind and fire.

But He protected us. One house fire is bad enough but there could have been six. My youngest lost her house but her son had been asleep in the house before the fire that threatened our houses. Perhaps coming to see about us is what saved him.

I believe that pleading the blood of Jesus over our houses and then beginning to praise the Lord for whatever happened opened the portal for angels to work on our behalf. At any rate, we give Him and some wonderful volunteer firemen all the glory and gratitude.

James 1:2 "Consider it pure joy, my brothers and sisters, whenever you face trials of many kinds, because you know that the testing of your faith produces perseverance."

Have you ever thought that when Jesus said, "No man can know the day or the hour when the Son shall return," it was because the date and time are different all over the world? He did however, emphasize, "Watch, be ready."

KNOW THE ENEMY!

The devil walks about as a roaring lion, seeking whom he may devour. Often, the enemy attacks our mind, planting worries and fears. That's why Elijah ran from Jezebel, even though he had just made a mockery of the prophets of Baal on Mt. Carmel, God sending down fire and having them killed. But, for some reason, Jezebel got power over Elijah's mind. She threatened him and he ran.

"Afraid of Fear"

I couldn't get a breath. For two nights I had stayed up trying to overcome the panic attack. I could not breathe. The cancerous spot on my nose had not bothered me. I had cancelled the surgery to remove it and I had not even told my family about it because I didn't want them to worry. I was doing all of the alternative procedures I could find and I just knew that it would go away soon.

Then, one evening, I felt a growth inside my nose and I began to think about my nose closing up and not being able to breathe. I prayed to God and I talked to myself all day and all night. But in the middle of the second night, I simply could not breathe. I knew it was an anxiety attack because I had gone to the hospital once before with the same symptoms.

I had never been able to breathe very well and I remember, as a child, feeling like I could breathe better when I was at the city swimming pool. But claustrophobia, the fear of closed spaces, started when I was in elementary school.

Some friends and I had gone to the creek gulley where I had often gone to explore. I had once found a snake there and put it in a jar to take home with me. I forgot to punch holes in the lid and the snake was dead by the time I got home. When my sisters and I were getting ready to have a funeral for the snake, my mother looked at it and very calmly told me, "You can be grateful he suffocated. That was a poisonous water moccasin."

This summer day my friends were with me and I had to think of something more adventurous than finding snakes, so I suggested that we crawl through the cement pipe that went through the hill and underneath the railroad tracks. Being the daredevil leader of the bunch, I crawled in first with five or six kids coming in right behind me. The pipe was longer than we thought and there was only room to crawl single file. It seemed like it was taking forever and the dirt was sifting down from cracks in the old pipe. It was getting hard to breathe. I couldn't wait to get to the other end and get out of there. Then I saw a horrible sight. The pipe was completely clogged up with dirt and you couldn't get through. I screamed, "Back up! Back up!" There was not enough room to turn around and it took everyone so long to back out of that tiny cement trap that I thought I would never get out.

Since that time I've tried to avoid any enclosed spaces. Even elevators were hard for me because I knew that they could get stuck. Once, going up the Arch in St. Louis, when they closed the stainless steel door and four of us were squashed knee to knee, I told those with me, "If this stops and the door doesn't open, knock me out quickly or I will kill everyone." I walked all the way back down the Arch.

Although I had always loved flying, I wanted to stop flying because the seats were so crowded. When the passenger in front of me leaned back, he was in my lap. I had read twice about a plane sitting on the tarmac for hours without letting the passengers deplane. Those would have been dangerous situations had I been on those planes. When I read about the incidents, I thought, "I would have gone nuts. I can't take a chance of that happening." So I decided to stop flying.

But now I was flying down the road and to the hospital.

Although four of my children live on the same road, I did not want to disturb them. I figured that at the emergency room they would give me a shot and I could come back home. I drove the fifteen miles to the hospital thinking only of being able to breathe. I had actually gone to the emergency room that day but it was so full of people with serious injuries that I left and went back home, determined to overcome my anxiety.

At the emergency room, I told them I couldn't breathe, that I was having a panic attack. They wanted to make sure it wasn't a heart attack, so they kept me all night and the next day to run tests. I called one of my daughters to tell her that I wouldn't be at game night. She asked, "Where are you?" When I said, "In the hospital," she screamed, "You're where? We'll be right there." And they were and I got the scolding of my life.

After they had calmed down, we tried to figure out where to go to find out about the growth in my nose and to remove the carcinoma on top. We ended up going to doctors in Dallas who said that the growth inside was not the cancer growing through but only a polyp and could be easily removed. The day after the surgery, I felt so well, that I rearranged my furniture. That night, I called a daughter when I awoke bleeding from my mouth and nose.

Strangling and choking on my own blood, they rushed me to the hospital again, where the doctors packed one of my nostrils. Later, I went to another emergency room because my throat was closing up on me. The next three months were a horrible nightmare, going from doctor to doctor, surgery after surgery. I knew it was all my fear of not being able to breathe.

I hated for my children to have to do so much for me but I was very grateful for them. "Lord, thank you for my children taking care of me, taking turns staying every night." But I was embarrassed that it was necessary.

I had gone from a healthy woman who never went to doctors, never took medicine to a person whose calendar was filled with doctors' appointments and whose purse was filled with pills.

"Lord, how do I overcome this fear?" I asked over and over. And I have another mission trip coming up.

"I just cannot go on this next mission trip. We will be on six airplanes, as well as buses and vans. What if I can't get close to a door? What if I can't get an aisle seat? What if I have a panic attack in a foreign country? I don't want to take a chance. I really don't want to go. Maybe something will happen and I won't be able to go."

"Lord, so many people are battling so much cancer and other illnesses, I am such a coward. Please help me. How can I pray for others if I cannot believe for my own healing?"

But I have learned a lot through all of this:

It is easier to pray for others and believe than it is for myself.

It is easier to give advice when I haven't been there myself.

Doctors, hospitals, and medicine are blessings. Forgive me for all the words I've spoken against them.

"Forgive me for my pride when I have never gone through what others have suffered."

"Despise not the chastening of the Lord; neither be weary of his correction: for whom the Lord loves he corrects. Prov.3:12

I went on the mission trip, flew on six planes, didn't always get aisle seats, didn't always get front seats on the buses, but I got so busy praying and trying to help that my breathing problem was almost forgotten. If it popped into my mind, I claimed the verses that the Lord had shown me and I commanded the spirit of fear to leave me.

"I sought the Lord and he heard me and delivered me from all my fears." Ps. 34:4

"What time I am afraid, I will trust in thee." Ps. 56:3

"Behold, God is my salvation; I will trust, and not be afraid." Isaiah 12:3

REALIZE HOW MUCH GOD LOVES YOU!

God loved us so much that he sent His only son to die a cruel death for us. What kind of love is that? That God would come to earth, lay down his life as a payment for our sins, and promise to come back so that we could be His bride and live with Him eternally?

"Unfailing Love"

Jesus has revealed many things about himself to me. Every day He shows His love for me but I shall never forget the day that I was just bent over on the floor, crying because of my sinfulness. I felt like the most dismal failure in the world and I proceeded to tell the Father that I couldn't see how He could possibly love and forgive me. I was such a terrible person.

Suddenly, in my mind's eye, I saw Jesus. He lifted me up off the floor and placed me against his heart and He spoke to me, saying, "You don't belong down there. You belong here." He told me precious things and over and over He told me of His love.

Then He told me to open my Bible. It fell open to Psalms 31. I read along and recognized a term that I had not really picked up on before, "His unfailing love." I thought, "That's neat," and went on reading. The next Psalm also mentioned, "His unfailing love," and the Psalm after that, Psalm 33, mentioned it three times.

I said, "Lord, are you trying to tell me something?"

He reminded me of a song that He had given me several months before:

"I want to praise and magnify your name,
I want to praise and magnify your holy name,
With **unfailing love** you sought me,
With your precious blood you bought me,
I will praise and magnify your name."

Now, it is strange that we can sing something and read something many times and not really comprehend it. But the next thing He spoke into my spirit blew me away.

"I kissed your eyes as you slept,
So that your sleep was sweet,
I washed your world with rain,
So that it would gleam and sparkle.
I kissed your lips and whispered, 'You are mine,'
And now I tell you over and over,
Of my unfailing love.
Go in peace,
Knowing that no good thing will I withhold."

I will always remember that God not only answers our prayers, but, if we will listen, He will speak to us and tell us of His unfailing love. Thank you, Father, for speaking to us and for all those who want to hear.

Jeremiah 29:13 "And you shall seek me, and find me, when you shall search for me with all your heart."

"Now also when I am old and gray-headed, O God, forsake me not; until I have shown your strength to this generation, and your power to everyone that is to come." Psalm 71:18